HEINEMANN
STATE STUDIES

Illinois
Native Peoples

Andrew Santella

Heinemann Library
Chicago, Illinois

Customer Service 888-454-2279

Visit our website at www.heinemannlibrary.com

Designed by Heinemann Library
Page layout by Depke Design
Printed and bound in the United States by Lake
Book Manufacturing, Inc.

07 06 05 04 03
10 9 8 7 6 5 4 3 2 1

**Library of Congress
Cataloging-in-Publication Data**
Santella, Andrew.
  Illinois native peoples / by Andrew Santella.
    v. cm. -- (State studies)
Includes bibliographical references and index.
Contents: Early native peoples -- Native Americans
and European contact
-- Native American ways of life -- Native American
beliefs -- Illinois tribes today.
  ISBN 1-40340-009-1 (HC), 1-40340-570-0 (PbK)
1. Indians of North America--Illinois--Juvenile
literature. [1. Indians of North America--Illinois.]
I. Title. II. State studies
(Heinemann Library (Firm))
  E78.I3 S26 2002
  977.3'00497--dc21

                                    2002000797

Some words are shown in
bold, **like this.** You can
find out what they mean
by looking in the glossary.

Acknowledgments
The author and publishers are grateful to the
following for permission to reproduce copyright material:

Cover photographs by (TL-TR): Warren Perlstein
Photography; North Wind Pictures; Courtesy of Cahokia
Mounds State Historic Site; (bottom) Warren Perlstein
Photography

p. 4 Bob and Ira Spring/Stock Connection/PictureQuest; pp. 5, 6,
15, 39 maps.com/Heinemann Library; p. 7T Jonathan Blair/
Corbis; p. 7B Carter Sisney Photography; p. 8T Western Illinois
University Archaeological Research Laboratory; pp. 8B, 9 Cahokia
Mounds State Historic Site; p. 10 "Man Who Tracks, a Chief," by
George Catlin. Gift of Mrs. Joseph Harrison, Jr., Smithsonian
American Art Museum, Washington, D.C. /Art Resource;
p. 11 North Wind Pictures; p. 12 The Ho-Chunk Nation; p. 13
"Wakusasse, a Fox Warrior." Gift of the Enron Art Foundation.
Joslyn Art Museum, Omaha, Nebraska; p. 14 Indian of the Nation
of Kaskaskia, from the atlas to Callot's "Voyage dans l'Amerique
Septenitrionale," 1826. Engraved by Tardieu. Library of Congress,
Washington, D.C./Bridgeman Art Library; p. 16 Color lithograph
by George Catlin, 1844 (based on a sketch by George Catlin in
the Fort Gibson area, 1834). Illinois State Museum, Springfield,
IL; p. 17 "Wabaunsee. Causer of Paleness" (Potawatomi chief),
by Charles Bird King. Oil on panel, 1835/The Granger Collection,
NY; p. 18 "Winnebago Chief Hoowanneka, or Little Elk."
Lithograph after a painting, 1826, by James Otto Lewis/The
Granger Collection, NY; p. 19 Gary Andrashko, Illinois State
Museum; p. 20 NAA, Smithsonian Institution, neg no. 94-7112;
p. 21 Engraving by Theodor de Bry (1528-1598), from "A briefe
and true report of the new found land of Virginia."/Bridgeman
Art Library; p. 22 Michelle Mouldenhauer, Archaeological Society
of Virginia; p. 23 Gary Andrashko. Illinois State Museum; p. 24
Robert Lifson/Heinemann Library; p. 25 N. Carter/North Wind
Pictures; p. 26 Marilyn "Angel" Wynn, Nativestock.com; p. 27T
North Wind Pictures; p. 27B "Keokuk (The Watchful Fox)," by
George Catlin. Gift of Mrs. Joseph Harrison, Jr., Smithsonian
American Art Museum, Washington, D.C. /Art Resource; p. 28
Prescription stick, Potawatomi, c. 1860, The Detroit Institute of
Arts/Bridgeman Art Library; p. 29 Gunter Max Photography/
Corbis; pp. 30, 33 The Detroit Institute of Arts; p. 31 American
engraving, after Seth Eastman, 1851/The Granger Collection, NY;
p. 32 North Wind Pictures; p. 34 Drawing of Piasa observed by
Jacques Marquette and Louis Jolliet on their 1673 voyage down
the Mississippi River. (From a map drawn by Franquelin,
1678)/French Naval Archives, Vincennes, France; p. 35T "Brewett.
A Celebrated Miami Chief. Taken at the Treaty of Massinnewa by
J.O. Lewis, 1827."/Marion Public Library, Marion, Indiana;
p. 35B Hulton Archive; p. 36 "Indian Burial at Kee-waw-nay, a
Potawatomi village, 1837." Watercolor by George Winter,
1863-1971. Gift of Mrs. Cable G. Ball/Tippecanoe County
Historical Association, Lafayette, Indiana; p. 37 NAA, Smithsonian
Institution, neg no. 54837; pp. 38, 41T Warren Perlstein
Photography; p. 40 Ho-Chunk Casino; p. 41B Sac & Fox Nation,
Stroud, Oklahoma; p. 42 Miami Tribe of Oklahoma, Miami,
Oklahoma; p. 43 Peoria Indian Tribe, Miami, Oklahoma;
p. 44 James P. Rowan.

Special thanks to Tom Schwartz of the Illinois
Historic Preservation Agency, for his expert help and
advice on the series.

Contents

Early Native Peoples

Native Americans were the first people to live in Illinois. When French explorers first reached the area in 1673, they were welcomed. Native Americans helped the explorers find their way through their territory. By the time the French arrived, native peoples had already been living in Illinois for about 12,000 years.

Native Americans were the first to farm Illinois's rich soil. They built the first villages along the rivers of Illinois. Even the state's name comes from Native Americans. Illinois is named for the Illinois Nation, a group of Native American tribes in the region.

*Glaciers (right) are huge sheets of ice and snow, sometimes as much as a mile thick, that move across land. Thousands of years ago, glaciers helped shape the landscape of Illinois. That last **Ice Age** ended about 11,500 years ago.*

Illinois

Most Native American groups believe their people were always in America. However, the first residents of America probably came from Asia. At least 14,000 years ago, they walked from Asia to North America. At that time, the two continents were connected by land, between what is today Alaska and Northeast Asia. Today, the "land bridge" that connected the two continents is covered by the Bering Sea. These early people were called Paleo-Indians, or "ancient Indians." Over thousands of years, the Paleo-Indians and their **descendants** spread out over North America.

Glaciers and the Bering Strait

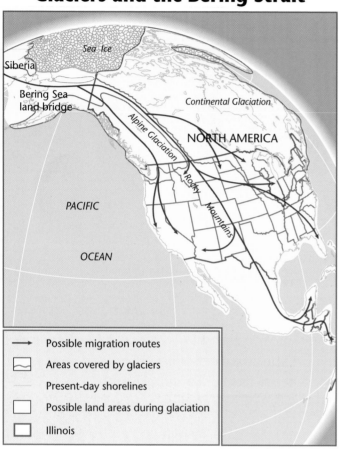

Most Native Americans believe their people have always been in the Americas. Evidence suggests that Paleo-Indians probably came from Asia, across the Bering Sea land bridge.

When Paleo-Indians arrived in the land that we call Illinois, the **climate** was cooler than it is today. Glaciers that had covered Illinois were retreating to the north as the temperature rose and they melted. Glaciers are huge sheets of ice and snow, sometimes as much as a mile thick, that move across land (see the photo on page 4). Animals that are now **extinct,** such as **mastodons** and **mammoths,** still lived in Illinois at that time. There were also animals that we would recognize, like squirrels and white-tailed deer. The Paleo-Indians survived by hunting animals and gathering wild plants. They were nomads, or people who moved from place to place in search of food.

The first people to farm in Illinois lived between 8000 and 1000 B.C.E. This was called the **Archaic Period.** They grew squash and gourds. Because they farmed, people of the Archaic Period did not have to depend as much on hunting for their food. They could also stay in one place and tend their crops.

Between 1000 B.C.E. and C.E. 800, people in Illinois began growing corn. This period was called the **Woodland Period.** Woodland people were also skilled makers of clay pottery. They mixed together clay and bits of crushed rock to form a paste. They shaped this paste into

*The woolly mammoth (left) is an extinct relative of the modern elephant. Some mammoths were more than 14 feet (4.3 meters) tall, with tusks 13 feet (4 meters) long. Their long hair helped protect them from the severe cold of the **Ice Age.***

bowls or other kinds of containers, then baked them in fires to harden them. Clay pottery made it much easier for Woodland people to store and cook food.

Illinois was a center for trade during the Woodland Period. Traders traveled great distances on the area's rivers,

Atlatl

The above photographs show an atlatl in use. People of the Archaic Period used atlatls for hunting. It helped hunters throw their spears greater distances and with more force. An atlatl was a wooden tool with a hooked end. The hunter placed one end of the spear in the hooked end of the atlatl. With a flick of the forearm, the hunter then launched the spear. Today, some athletes compete in atlatl events, including long-distance spear throwing.

Woodland people made clay pots in which they stored food. Before the Woodland Period, containers were made with wood, plants, or leather.

probably in canoes dug out of tree trunks. In Whiteside County in Northwest Illinois, **archaeologists** found seashells among the remains of one Woodland settlement. They could only have come from somewhere far away, like the Atlantic Ocean or Gulf of Mexico. This shows that trading took place over great distances.

MISSISSIPPI VILLAGES

About C.E. 900, native people in Illinois began building large villages. This was called the **Mississippian Period.** Most of these villages were along the Mississippi River. The largest was Cahokia. It may have been home to as many as 15,000 people. Houses at Cahokia were made up of one room, with a fireplace that was used for cooking. There were pits used to store food and platforms for sleeping in the same room.

People of the Mississippian Period built Monks Mound (below) in southern Illinois. The village leader or priest may have lived at the top of the mound.

At the center of Cahokia, there was a plaza and a huge mound that came to be known as Monks Mound. Monks Mound is the largest **prehistoric** structure still standing in what is now the United States. It is over 100 feet (30.5 meters) tall, 1,000 feet (305 meters) long, and 800 feet (244 meters) wide at its base. There was a large building at the top of the mound. This was perhaps the home of the most important priest or leader of the village. Monks Mound was the largest of many mounds built in the Mississippi River valley by these ancient people. There were more than 100 mounds at Cahokia alone. Some of these mounds were used as burial places.

Ancient Cahokia may have been home to as many as 15,000 people. Monks Mound sat at the center of the city, along with a large plaza (above).

About 700 years ago, the population of Cahokia and other neighboring villages began to decline. Changes in Illinois's **climate** may have worked to decrease their supply of food. Diseases or wars may have taken the lives of many Mississippian people. Whatever the reason, by about C.E. 1500, the Mississippian culture had disappeared from Illinois. When the first French explorers arrived in the area in the late 1600s, they found a different Native American culture.

European Contact

When French explorers reached Illinois in 1673, there were several groups of Native Americans living there. One group was the Miami people. They lived in villages along the shores of Lake Michigan. The other groups were part of the Illinois Nation. The Illinois Nation was made up of twelve independent tribes who shared a common language and had similar ways of life. The Illinois Nation is sometimes called a confederation. In a confederation, two or more groups join forces to protect each other against common enemies. The Illinois Nation lived along the Mississippi River and smaller rivers, from present-day Wisconsin in the north to present-day Arkansas in the South.

This is an 1830 painting of Pah-me-cow-e-tah (Man Who Tracks), a Peoria chief. The Peoria were part of the Illinois Confederacy.

The prairies and forests of Illinois provided everything the native people of the area needed. Both the Miami and the Illinois people grew corn, beans, squash, and other crops. They also hunted the plentiful deer, turkey, and **bison.** The great rivers of Illinois put them at the center of trade networks. However, those rivers also brought other people to their land, and those people brought great changes.

In the mid–1600s, Iroquois warriors invaded Illinois. Some native tribes were driven from their homelands, and others moved in to take their place. At about the same time, French traders and **missionaries** began exploring Illinois. Jacques Marquette and Louis Jolliet were the first French to visit in 1673. In the years that followed, several other Native American tribes moved into Illinois. These included the Sauk, Fox, Kickapoo, Potawatomi, Shawnee, and Winnebago. Some tribes moved to live closer to their French trading partners. Others came to make war on neighboring tribes.

To survive these changing times, Native Americans had to learn new ways of life. They became trading partners with the French, and

Tribes of the Illinois

Cahokia (ca-HO-ki-a)

Chepoussa (che-POUS-sa)

Chinko (CHIN-ko)

Coiracoentanon (coi-ra-coen-TAN-on)

Espeminkia (es-pe-MIN-ki-a)

Kaskaskia (kas-KAS-ki-a)

Michibousa (mich-i-BOU-sa)

Michigamea (mich-i-GA-me-a)

Moingwena (moin-GWE-na)

Peoria (pe-O-ri-a)

Tamaroa (ta-ma-RO-a)

Tapouaro (ta-POUA-ro)

Marquette and Jolliet (below) were the first Europeans to meet the Illinois people. A Native American from Illinois first told Marquette about the existence of the Mississippi River.

Buffalo Hunts

Most tribes in Illinois didn't acquire horses until the 1700s. So they learned to hunt buffalo, or **bison** (right), on foot, using bows and arrows. Some hunting parties tried to surround herds of buffalo. Others set fire to the prairie grass near the buffalo, hoping to drive them toward waiting hunters, who would shoot them down.

The buffalo provided Native Americans with food, shelter, and clothing. Native American women made robes out of buffalo hides. They turned buffalo bones into needles and knives. Native American women also cooked and preserved buffalo meat. Sometimes they roasted the meat over a fire. Other times, they dried the meat on racks to make it last a long time. Then they cut it into thin strips called jerky. One woman could prepare the meat of three buffalo in a single day—that's 300 pounds of buffalo meat!

later with the British and Americans. They helped white traders collect beaver **pelts** to be turned into hats and clothing in Europe. In return, European traders supplied them with guns, brass kettles, iron tools, and other trade goods. These were sometimes more effective and durable than the Native Americans' pottery and stone tools. Some tribes also adopted European ways of living. For example, by about 1700, the Kaskaskia began raising pigs, chickens, and other farm animals as the French did.

However, white traders and settlers also brought diseases that the Native Americans could not fight. They also helped start wars among the tribes. The combination of disease and warfare sometimes wiped out entire tribes. The following are the tribes, in alphabetical order, that once lived in what we now call Illinois:

CAHOKIA

The Cahokia were one of the tribes of the Illinois Nation. Like the other Illinois tribes, they spoke the Miami-Illinois language. They lived in southwestern Illinois, near where the Illinois River meets the Mississippi River. In 1752, the Fox and Shawnee attacked and destroyed the main Cahokia village. The surviving Cahokia left to live with their neighbors, the Michigamea. By 1800, only a few Cahokia survived. They became part of the Peoria tribe.

FOX

The Fox call themselves the *Mesquakie*, which means "red earth people." Their language is part of the Sauk-Fox group of the Algonquin language family. The Fox once lived in Wisconsin, but in the 1730s, they began invading the lands of the Illinois Nation. With their neighbors, the Sauk, they drove the Illinois tribes away. Some of the Fox settled along the Rock River in northern Illinois.

ILLINOIS NATION

The tribes of the Illinois Nation shared the same language, which is part of the Algonquin language family. Because this language is closely related to the language of the Miami, it is sometimes called Miami-Illinois. The name Illinois comes from a French spelling of their own name for themselves—*Illiniwek*. Roughly translated, *Illiniwek* means "the men" or "the people." The tribes of the Illinois Nation occupied a vast territory along the Mississippi River. They lived in Wisconsin, Iowa, Illinois, Missouri, and Arkansas. Only some of the Illinois tribes made their home in the land

This is Wakusasse, a Fox warrior. The headdress was made of deer and porcupine hair. It was meant to look like a woodpecker, which was a bird the Fox associated with war.

that would become the state of Illinois. These included the Cahokia, Kaskaskia, Michigamea, Peoria, and Tamaroa. For more information, read the separate entries for each of these tribes.

KASKASKIA

The Kaskaskia belonged to the Illinois Nation. Their name means "people who scrape with tools" in the Illinois language. They lived in a village of 1,200 people on the Illinois River, near today's Starved Rock State Park. Invading Iroquois drove them from this village in the 1670s. Illness and warfare killed many Kaskaskia over the next 100 years. By 1778, there were only about 200 Kaskaskia left. In 1828, the surviving Kaskaskia moved to Missouri as part of the Peoria tribe.

This is a drawing (below) of a member of the Kaskaskia tribe of Illinois in around 1826. There were very few Kaskaskia left at that time.

KICKAPOO

The Kickapoo language belongs to the Sauk-Fox group of the Algonquin language family. It is almost identical to the language of the Shawnee. Their name comes from *Kiwegapaw*, which in that language means "people who move about." In about 1716, they began invading the land of the Illinois Nation. With the Fox and Sauk, they drove away their neighbors to the south. They settled along the Wabash River in southeastern Illinois.

European Contact, 1650–1700

Map labels:

- Fox River
- Lake Michigan
- 1689–90
- Winnebago
- Fort Chicago 1680
- Fox
- Rock River
- Potawatomi
- MI
- 1687
- Iowa River
- 1690–95?
- MI
- MI
- MI, PO
- Sauk
- Kankakee River
- IL
- IL
- 1684
- Fort Pimitoui 1691
- Fort St. Louis 1682–91
- IL 1691
- Kickapoo
- Dickson Mounds
- Fort de Crèvecoeur 1680-80
- Mississippi River
- Illinois River
- Illinois
- Sangamon River
- Kaskaskia River
- Embarras River
- Wabash River
- 1680
- Missouri River
- IL
- IL, OT, TI
- IL
- Cahokia Mounds
- IL
- Big Muddy River
- Shawnee
- Ohio River
- N W E S
- 0   100 mi.
- 0   100 km

Legend:

→ Route of Marquette and Jolliet, 1673	⬯ Prehistoric mound sites
● Iroquois victory	🐦 Native American village at some time during this period
✕ Iroquois defeat	■ Fort
1660 Date established, occupied beyond 1701	IL Illinois
1682-91 Dates established and abandoned	MI Miami
Fox Rough location of tribe	PO Potawatomi

Most Native American tribes did not always stay in one particular place. However, this map gives a rough idea of where different tribes could be found in Illinois in the late 1600s. It also shows prehistoric sites and European exploration and settlements.

MIAMI

The Miami take their name from an Ojibwa word, *Oumamik*, which means "people of the peninsula." They once lived near present-day Green Bay, Wisconsin. In the mid–1600s, they began moving south and settled along the southern shores of Lake Michigan, near present-day Chicago. Around 1700, they spread east across Indiana and into Ohio. The Miami were made up of six bands, or groups. Two of those bands, the Piankashaw and the Wea, became independent tribes by 1818. They both settled in southeastern Illinois.

MICHIGAMEA

The Michigamea belonged to the Illinois Nation. They once lived along the Sangamon River in central Illinois. In 1673, the French explorers Jacques Marquette and Louis Jolliet met them in southern Missouri. Around 1720, they moved to a village next to the French Fort de Chartres, near Prairie du Rocher in southwest Illinois. Like the other Illinois tribes, their population fell in the 1700s. The surviving members of the tribe joined other Illinois tribes.

Lacrosse

Many Native American tribes played lacrosse (right). Some games could involve hundreds of players and might last for days. The people of the Illinois Nation played a version that often included both men and women. Teams used stringed rackets to carry or throw a ball toward a goal. The racket

strings were made of animal **sinew.** The ball was made of wood. The goal consisted of two upright poles placed ten paces apart in the middle of the field. Games often matched two villages or tribes against each other. The contests could be very rough and dangerous. To some Native American warriors, lacrosse was considered a form of battle.

PEORIA

The Peoria were one of the main tribes of the Illinois Nation. The Peoria lived in southern Wisconsin, eastern Iowa, and northern Illinois. They settled along the Illinois River, near present-day Peoria, Illinois, in the late 1600s. There they lived in close contact with their French trading partners. Attacks by the Fox and other neighboring tribes drove them west across the Mississippi River in 1769. Today, the Peoria tribe of Oklahoma represents all the **descendants** of the Illinois Nation.

POTAWATOMI

The Potawatomi were one of the strongest tribes of northern Wisconsin. They are closely related to the Ottawa and Ojibwa. Their name means "people of the place of the fire" in Ojibwa. In the early 1700s, they moved south to take over lands once held by the Illinois Nation and the Miami. They lived along the shores of Lake Michigan, between present-day Milwaukee, Wisconsin, and present-day Chicago. They also hunted across much of northern Illinois.

SAUK

The Sauk call themselves *Osakiwug*, which means "people of the yellow earth." In the 1730s, they joined with the Fox to invade the lands of the Illinois Nation. They settled in northern Illinois, near the Rock River. In 1832, a Sauk war chief named Black Hawk led the last resistance to white settlers in Illinois. He and his band of Sauk and Fox warriors were defeated in a war that came to be called the Black Hawk War (1832). Young Abraham Lincoln volunteered to serve in the Black Hawk War, though he didn't fight in any battles.

Waubonsee (above) was an important member of the Potawatomi tribe in northern Illinois. The Potawatomi came south from Wisconsin in the early 1700s.

SHAWNEE

Close relatives of the Fox, Sauk, and Kickapoo, the Shawnee lived in the Ohio River valley. The Shawnee and the Kickapoo believe they were once part of the same tribe, which split into two after a disagreement. The languages of the two tribes are almost the same.

In the 1600s, some Shawnee bands moved into southern Illinois to hunt and settle near French trading posts.

TAMAROA

The Tamaroa were part of the Illinois Nation. They lived in southwestern Illinois, between the Kaskaskia and Illinois Rivers. Like other tribes of the Illinois Nation, the Tamaroa population declined in the 1700s. The remaining members of the tribe joined the Kaskaskia and Peoria by 1800.

WINNEBAGO

Unlike most Native American tribes of Illinois, the Winnebago spoke a language of the Siouan language family. The Winnebago lived in eastern Wisconsin in the 1600s, but later moved west and south into Illinois. They established villages along the Rock River. In 1832, some Winnebago took part in the Black Hawk War, the last war between natives and white settlers in Illinois. Today, some Winnebago call themselves the Ho-Chunk Nation, which means "people of the first voice" in their language.

Hoowanneka (left), or Little Elk, was a Winnebago chief. Winnebago chiefs could also be women. The Winnebago lost their land in Illinois in the 1830s.

Ways of Life

Many Native American ways of life in Illinois were very connected to the natural world. Before the arrival of Europeans, the natural world provided Native Americans with everything they needed to live. They lived in homes made of wood and plant material from Illinois forests. Their diet was a mix of crops grown in the Illinois soil and meat gathered by hunters on the prairies. Even their tools were made of stone, wood, and animal bone that could be found close to home.

The tribes that lived in and around Illinois shared many ways of life. Most depended on both hunting and farming for food. They also divided the tribe's tasks among men and women. Women usually tended the crops. The basic crops for most tribes of the area were corn, beans, squash, and melons. Men hunted for **bison** and other animals. Women cleaned and prepared the meat and made robes and other clothing from animal hides.

The tribes of Illinois used almost every part of the animals they hunted. Below is an engraved Kaskaskia arrow-shaft wrench made of a bison rib (top). Below that (bottom) is a hoe (device used for digging and scraping dirt) made from the shoulder blade of a bison, which would have been attached to a wood handle.

Women also built houses made of wooden poles and woven **rush** mats. Men were hunters, traders, and warriors. They were responsible for making and repairing weapons, canoes, and other tools needed for their work.

Fox

In the warmest months of the year, the Fox lived in villages made up of large lodges. Each lodge housed as many as 30 people. They were made of wooden frames covered with the bark of elm trees. There were garden plots outside each village, which the tribe's women usually tended. In late fall and winter, the Fox moved to temporary camps for their yearly **bison** hunt. Unlike neighboring tribes, the Fox did not break into small groups for their winter hunts. Instead, they stayed in large village units. However, their winter homes were smaller and might be left behind when the tribe moved to another location. The Fox were governed by chiefs and a **council** of **elders.** The elders represented each of the Fox **clans.** Some chiefs were chosen based on their wisdom and **spiritual** power. In other cases, leadership was passed from father to son. The Fox chose their war leaders based on bravery and skill.

This photograph from the 1800s shows a Winnebago woman softening a deer hide that has been stretched across a wooden frame. Next she will sew it into a bag and smoke it until she gets the desired color.

Canoes

All of the tribes that lived in Illinois used canoes. Some used birchbark canoes. These were made of a wood frame with sheets of bark from birch trees stretched over it. They were light enough for a single person to carry. These were popular with tribes that once lived in the forests of Michigan and Wisconsin, where birch trees were plentiful. The tribes of the Illinois Nation used dugout canoes (right).

These were made by burning or chopping out the trunk of a tree to form the canoe. Instead of paddling dugout canoes, the Illinois often used long poles to push off from the shore or the river bottom.

ILLINOIS NATION

The tribes of the Illinois Nation included the Cahokia, Chepoussa, Chinko, Coiracoentanon, Espeminkia, Kaskaskia, Michibousa, Michigamea, Moingwena, Peoria, Tamaroa, and Tapouaro. The Illinois almost always made their villages next to rivers. They could usually find good land there for farming. The main crop of the Illinois was corn. They planted corn in the spring and harvested it in July and August. They stored extra corn in pits to use during the winter. They also gathered nuts and wild fruit. In the spring, they tapped maple trees for sugar and syrup.

Rivers also made it easy for the Illinois to trade with neighboring tribes. They traveled hundreds of miles in dugout canoes. The Illinois often traded with the Potawatomi for porcupine **quills.** They were more easily gathered in Potawatomi territory, and the Illinois used them to decorate their clothes.

The Illinois lived in lodges, or longhouses. These houses were usually around 60 feet (18 meters) long. They were made of wood poles covered with layers of mats woven from **rushes** and long grasses. They housed as many as ten families. Inside, the house was divided into rooms, with a fireplace for each family. In the winter, the Illinois broke up into smaller villages. Each winter village might contain ten or twenty **wigwams.** Wigwams were smaller than summer lodges but made with the same materials. They were usually about ten to twenty feet (three to six meters) wide.

The Illinois depended on buffalo, or **bison,** hunting more than most of their neighbors. Each village went on a yearly buffalo hunt in June. They hunted the buffalo on foot, using bows and arrows with stone tips.

Illinois clothing was mostly made of skins from deer and bison. Men wore **breechcloths** and moccasins.

The Illinois tribes lived in longhouses (left) in the summer, and wigwams (right) in the winter. Both types of house were made of wood poles covered with layers of woven mats. Longhouses were divided into rooms, with a fire pit for each family.

Illinois men sometimes wore long necklaces made of woven bison fur and decorated with feathers, brass cones, deer hair, and porcupine quills (left).

Women wore knee-length skirts and deerskin cloaks. Both men and women decorated themselves with tattoos and body paint. They wore jewelry made of polished stone and animal teeth.

Tribes of the Illinois Nation were governed by peace chiefs who directed hunts and handled relations with other tribes. War chiefs led attacks on other tribes and defended the villages. Among the Illinois, women sometimes acted as tribal leaders. Of all the tribes in the area, the Illinois had the closest relationship with French traders and settlers. The Illinois sometimes built their villages near French **forts** and trading posts. This was also because the French promised to protect the Illinois from their enemies. French priests tried to convert the Illinois to **Christianity.** Some Illinois did actually accept Christianity.

KASKASKIA

The main village of the Kaskaskia was at the meeting of the Illinois and Vermillion Rivers. It consisted of 74 lodges. Each was up to 100 feet (30.5 meters) long and housed as many as 6 families. In 1680, about 6,000 people lived in the village, including members of other Illinois tribes. As part of the Illinois Nation, the Kaskaskia shared many ways of life with other Illinois tribes.

KICKAPOO

The Kickapoo lived in the same, set villages during the warm-weather months. Their homes were oval-shaped.

Fort Dearborn

HERE·STOOD
OLD·FORT·DEARBORN
1803 – 1812

In 1812, war broke out between the United States and Great Britain. Some Native American tribes sided with the British. They were hoping to stop the flow of American settlers into their lands. On August 15, 1812, about 500 warriors from the Potawatomi, Kickapoo, Sauk, and Winnebago tribes attacked Fort Dearborn, at Chicago. They surprised a group of soldiers and settlers who were trying to leave the **fort.** Eighty-two people died in the battle that followed. The attack became known as the "Fort Dearborn Massacre." For a short time, it left the British and their Native American **allies** in control of northern Illinois.

They were made of a frame of green saplings, which are young trees, and covered with tree bark. After they gathered the harvest in the fall, the Kickapoo went on a buffalo, or **bison,** hunt. At their hunting camps, they built smaller, short-term houses. The Kickapoo were one of the first tribes in the area to use horses to hunt buffalo.

Kickapoo society was divided into **clans.** Children became members of their father's clan. Marriages were between two people from different clans. Clans also competed in sporting events, such as **lacrosse** games.

MIAMI

Miami society was divided into clans. Children became members of their father's clan. Marriages were always between two people from different clans. Leaders from each clan made up village **councils.** The village council elected one person as chief of the village.

Each village belonged to one of six bands, or groups. Each band had its own chief and council, as well. Finally, there was a large tribal council, made of representatives from all the clans and bands.

Miami men wore deerskin shirts, **moccasins,** and **breechcloths.** Women wore deerskin skirts and loose shirts or gowns. Both men and women decorated their bodies with tattoos. They wore jewelry made of polished colored stone and animal teeth.

Miami villages contained houses made of wood frames covered with mats made from grasses and **rushes.** They also contained community gardens. The Miami were known for the high quality of their white corn. It was highly prized by other tribes that the Miami traded with. The Miami also traded with both the French and the British. By the late 1700s, some Miami built log houses like those of the British and French. Some also began to wear European-style clothing.

POTAWATOMI

The Potawatomi lived in villages along streams, usually with an open field nearby. On this field, they played

Most tribes of Illinois, including the Potawatomi, grew what is known as the "three sisters," which are corn, beans, and squash. Traditionally, the three crops were grown together in the same area, as in this photograph (left). Each plant helps the others grow.

Native American Children in Illinois

Native American tribes in Illinois taught their children the skills they would need as adults. Boys learned to use bows and arrows to hunt. Girls were given dolls made of cornhusks (right) and helped their mothers with cooking, sewing, and other tasks. Teenage boys in the Fox, Shawnee, and

other tribes went through **vision quests** as part of growing up. In a vision quest, a boy would go off on his own and **fast** for several days. By fasting, he hoped to invite visions from the spirits. He might also perform dangerous acts, like diving into icy water. He prayed to his guardian spirit to lead him to manhood.

Girls did not perform vision quests. They did perform certain actions as part of the passage to adulthood. When a girl became a teenager, she might leave her village to live by herself for several days. She was then visited by older women from the village, who helped teach her about life as a woman. Girls also learned how to receive suitors, or young men who wished to marry them. When she returned from this time away, a girl was then considered a woman.

lacrosse and other games. Each village was governed by a chief and a **council** of **elders.** Potawatomi divided themselves into about 30 **clans.** Children became members of their father's clan. Marriages were always between two people of different clans. When a couple married, the man moved in with his wife's family.

Their homes were long lodges made of wooden poles covered with mats of long grasses and **rushes.** In the autumn, they gathered beechnuts that they pounded into flour. After the autumn harvest, they broke into smaller groups to hunt **bison** and other animals through the winter. In the spring, the Potawatomi gathered maple sap to be boiled into syrup and sugar.

Besides corn, beans, and squash, the Potawatomi also grew gardens of **herbs** used to treat illnesses and injuries.

Even members of other tribes came to the Potawatomi for treatment. The Potawatomi were also known for their skill in building birchbark canoes. They used their canoes to travel on local rivers and on Lake Michigan. Potawatomi women were skilled pottery makers.

SAUK

Sauk villages could be large enough to hold 1,000 warriors and their families. One summer village contained about 100 lodges. Sauk lodges were made of wood-pole frames covered with sheets of elm bark. Each one was about 50 feet (15 meters) long and housed several families. Inside were fireplaces and pits for storing food. In the winter, the Sauk built short-term villages in sheltered locations, like river valleys. Unlike neighboring tribes, they did not break into small groups for their winter hunt.

Sauk society was made up of twelve **clans.** Children became members of their father's clan. Sauk children were named by clan **elders** at a special naming **ceremony.** The Sauk were governed by a **council** of chiefs, whose jobs were passed from father to son. There were three kinds of chiefs. Civil chiefs handled everyday matters and settled arguments. Ceremonial chiefs led during special occasions like feasts. War chiefs led attacks on other

This is a wooden Potawatomi prescription stick made around 1860. Certain plants used for healing are engraved on the stick. Each group of plants is a particular healing recipe.

Black Hawk and Keokuk

Native Americans responded to the power of white settlers in different ways. Black Hawk (right) was a Sauk war chief who led the last Native American resistance in Illinois. In 1832, he led a group of Sauk and Fox warriors, women, and children from Iowa into the Rock River area of northwest Illinois. They wanted to plant crops there, as they had for centuries. The Illinois state government believed that the Sauk and Fox had promised to give up their land in Illinois. They tried to drive Black Hawk and his followers out. Black Hawk won one battle against state troops, but later his people had to flee into Wisconsin. Many of Black Hawk's people were killed in the Battle of Bad Axe as they tried to cross the Mississippi River into the West. Black Hawk surrendered and was imprisoned for a short time. The following year he

published his life story, which became an important work.

Another Sauk leader took a different approach. Keokuk (left) tried to remain friendly with white leaders. He gave up Sauk and Fox lands in Illinois and led his followers to Iowa. When Black Hawk led his uprising, Keokuk tried to warn white settlers. White leaders rewarded Keokuk by treating him as the head of all Sauk and Fox. He is the only Native American honored with a bronze sculpture in the United States Capitol.

tribes and defended Sauk villages. The Sauk also had a principal chief, who always came from the Sturgeon clan. The Sauk were split into two divisions—black and white. The divisions competed against each other in **lacrosse** games.

When the Sauk moved to northwest Illinois, they began mining lead. They melted it down and used it to make jewelry and other objects. Lead jewelry was an important trade item for the Sauk. They traded it to other tribes for furs and other goods.

SHAWNEE

The Shawnee lived in villages with fields nearby for growing corn. Their houses were made of wood-pole frames covered with sheets of bark. In the winter, they broke into smaller groups and lived in hunting camps.

The Shawnee were split into five major divisions. Each Shawnee was also a member of a clan. Membership in the clan was passed on from father to child. They were governed by peace chiefs and war chiefs. The job of peace chief, or civil chief, was passed on from father to son. War chiefs were chosen based on their bravery and skill in battle.

The Winnebago sometimes lived in tepees (above), which were actually more common among Great Plains tribes. The Winnebago used them for short-term camping on hunting trips.

WINNEBAGO

Winnebago houses were different from the longhouses most of their neighbors lived in. The Winnebago lived in dome-shaped houses called **wigwams.** Wigwams were made with small, thin trees, or saplings, covered with woven grasses. The Winnebago also sometimes lived in

tepees. Tepees were common among tribes of the Great Plains, just west of the Mississippi River. The Winnebago used them for short-term camping on hunting trips. Unlike most other tribes that lived in Illinois, they did not break into small groups for the winter. Instead, they lived in large village groups.

The Winnebago were made up of twelve **clans.** Each Winnebago became a member of his or her father's clan. Some clans performed special functions, like settling arguments. The principal chief of the Winnebago always came from the Thunderbird clan. The chief led along with a **council** of **elders** from each clan.

The Winnebago also split into two divisions. The Upper (or Sky) division was made up of four clans. The Lower (or Earth) division was made up of eight clans.

The Winnebago wore clothes made of animal furs and skins. They decorated them with beautiful designs made with feathers, beads, and porcupine **quills.** They were famous for their skill in decorating clothing.

The Winnebago were known for their skill in decorating clothing. This Winnebago man's shirt (right) was made around 1880. By the 1800s, tribes often mixed their traditional materials with new ones they obtained through trading with the Europeans. This shirt has wool fabric, silk ribbon, velvet ribbon, and glass beads.

Beliefs

Religious beliefs were a part of everyday life for Native Americans. Native Americans believed that spirits lived in the world around them and helped shape their lives. They performed **rituals** to win the favor of these spirits. A warrior would seek the help of spirits before he went into battle. A farming village would ask spirits to deliver a good harvest. Sick people might go to a **shaman,** or priest, seeking a cure from the spirits.

The tribes in Illinois shared some religious beliefs. For example, most of them believed in one supreme being that watched over the world. When French **missionaries** came to Illinois in the 1600s, they tried to convert Native Americans to **Christianity.** Some Native Americans did become Christians. Others kept their tribal beliefs.

Fox

The Fox believed that the world was split into two divisions. The Upper World was ruled by the Great Manitou,

*Medicine men, or shamans, used traditional methods to cure a patient. They would use **herbal** medicines and **ceremonies** to communicate with the spirits and pray for healing. This shaman (left) is using a sacred rattle in a healing ceremony.*

or Great Spirit. The Lower World was ruled by many lesser spirits. The Fox believed spirits existed in all things, from trees, to animals, to the sky. They also believed that each of the four directions—North, South, East, and West—had its own spirit. The East was the Land of the Sun, which brings life. The West was the Land of Departed Spirits, where people go after they die. The South belonged to the God of Thunder. The North was ruled by Wisaka, the Supreme Being. Like other tribes around the Great Lakes, the Fox had a Great Medicine Society, or *Midewiwin*. This was a secret religious group made up of believers with special **spiritual** powers. The members of the *Midewiwin* were the priests, or **shamans,** of the tribe. They appealed to the spirits for help for their people.

ILLINOIS NATION

The supreme being in the Illinois religion was the Master of Life, or *Kitchesmanetoa* (kitch-es-man-e-TO-a). The Illinois believed he existed in the sun and in thunder. They divided the universe into three worlds. The Upper World was the land of gods, including the Master of Life. The Middle World was the home of people and animals. The Lower World was the home of monsters. Each member of an Illinois tribe also prayed to a personal spirit, or *manitou*. Boys went on **vision quests** hoping to communicate with these spirits. Like other tribes in the area, the Illinois buried their dead in graves covered with wood. They also buried jewelry and other important objects the person could take with him or her to the afterlife.

KICKAPOO

The supreme being of the Kickapoo was *Kichiata*. The Kickapoo believed he created the world and lived in the sky. They believed that other spirits lived in all things. Each **clan** of the Kickapoo kept its own **sacred bundles.**

The Thunderbird spirit is found in rock art, on clothing, and on things such as this Fox bag from about 1850 (left). Tribes believed the Thunderbird caused thunder and lightning.

Sacred bundles were animal-skin pouches that contained objects representing glorious moments in the history of the clan and tribe. At a special **ceremony** each spring, the Kickapoo opened the sacred bundles and prayed for a renewal of past glories. The Kickapoo buried their dead in wooden containers or in hollow logs. The dead person was buried dressed in traveling clothes, with his or her feet pointed toward the West. The Kickapoo believed the West was the land of the departed. They buried food and water for the dead person to take on the journey.

The Piasa

On his first trip to Illinois in 1673, Jacques Marquette saw something strange. It was a huge painting of a monster on a Mississippi River cliff, near present-day Alton, Illinois. The painting had been made by people of the Illinois Nation. It showed the *Piasa* (Pie-ah-saw), one of the monsters they believed lived in the Lower World. Marquette said, "this winged monster

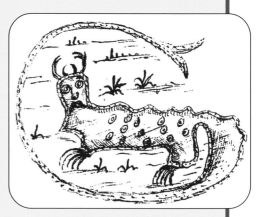

was as large as a calf, had horns like a deer, a horrible look, red eyes, a beard like a tiger's, a face somewhat like a man's, a body covered with scales, and a tail so long that it winds all around the body. . . ." The painting was later destroyed by white settlers. Today, a new *Piasa* painting can be seen on that cliff.

MIAMI

The Miami worshipped the Master of Life, who was represented by the sun. They had a Great Medicine Society, or *Midewiwin*, made up of people with special **spiritual** powers. The priests, or **shamans,** of the Great Medicine Society could get help from the spirits to cure the sick or defeat the Miami's enemies. The Miami used roots and **herbs** to help cure the sick, too. Much like the Kickapoo, **sacred bundles** were an important part of Miami **ceremonies.** These were animal-skin pouches filled with objects from the tribe's past. In the fall, the Miami celebrated the harvest with a feast. They held another feast to celebrate their return from the winter hunt. In this feast they played games, drummed, and danced.

POTAWATOMI

The Potawatomi believed in a Great Chain of Being that connected the past, present, and future. Their priests, or shamans, were also members of a Great Medicine Society, or *Midewiwin*. The shaman led the tribe in ceremonies to seek help from the spirits. Members of the tribe **fasted** in hopes of communicating with the spirits. Each clan of the tribe gathered for a naming ceremony for babies. On the baby's first birthday, **elders** and parents chose a name for the child. The Potawatomi believed the spirits of the dead went to live in the West. Most Potawatomi buried the dead in wooden containers. However, one **clan** burned the bodies of their dead.

SAUK

The Sauk believed in several spirits. The most important was *Wisaka.* Other spirits included South Wind, Fire, and Earth. The Sauk held festivals to celebrate the planting of crops in the spring and gathering of crops in the fall. There was also a festival celebrating the winter hunt. When they gathered plants or cut trees, they practiced a ceremony of apology for taking that life.

This drawing of a Miami chief (above) was done in 1827. As they traded with white settlers, Miami adopted some of their clothing. Most Miami kept their traditional beliefs though.

The Calumet

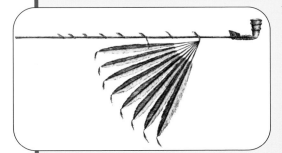

The Illinois and Miami both smoked a long tobacco pipe called a calumet (left) at special ceremonies. If leaders of two tribes met to settle a disagreement, they would smoke the calumet as a sign of peace. The calumet was also used as a sign of welcome to strangers.

The bowl of the pipe was made of hardened clay. The stem was made of wood, and was often decorated with eagle feathers.

The Potawatomi buried their dead in wooden containers. This is a traditional Potawatomi burial scene (above). They believed the spirits of the dead went to live in the West.

The Sauk believed a person's soul makes a journey after death. The soul must make its way past a guardian spirit and his watch dog before entering the land of the dead. Mourners blackened their faces with charcoal after a person's death.

SHAWNEE

The Shawnee worshipped a Supreme Being called *Moneto*, and a female Great Spirit called *Kokumthena*, which means "Our Grandmother." The Shawnee believed Kokumthena created them and would bring them to heaven. They also believed lesser spirits lived in all things. The Shawnee prayed for forgiveness when they took animal or plant life. They also kept **sacred bundles,** which were very important. Each sacred bundle held objects that represented the tribe's history. In sacred bundle **ceremonies,** the Shawnee asked for help curing the sick, winning battles, or gathering a good harvest. One of their most important festivals was the Spring Bread Dance. At this festival, the Shawnee honored their women for their farming skills and prayed for protection for their crops. Teams of men and women competed in ball games at the spring festival. Shawnee children were named ten days after they were born. A **clan elder** helped the parents choose a name related to the name of their clan. For example, a member of the Horse Clan might be named Swift Horse.

WINNEBAGO

The Winnebago worshipped several spirits. The most powerful was named Earthmaker. Other spirits included Thunderbird and Morning Star. Morning Star gave blessings for war. The Winnebago believed that a spirit named Disease-giver both gave and took life. They also formed societies to worship individual spirits. For example, the Buffalo Society worshipped the Buffalo Spirit. They made gifts for the Buffalo Spirit and asked for his blessing. Two of the most important Winnebago festivals were the Medicine Dance and the Winter Feast. The Medicine Dance was held in the summer. It was led by members of the Great Medicine Society, which was open to both men and women. At the Winter Feast, the Winnebago asked the spirits to give them power in war and hunting.

These Winnebago are carrying decorated medicine pouches made of beaver fur. They are leaving a Midewiwin lodge after the end of a Great Medicine Dance in 1896.

Illinois Tribes Today

Illinois became a state in 1818. By that time, many of the Native American groups that once lived in Illinois had disappeared. Some tribes died out as a result of wars and illnesses brought by white settlers. Others were driven from their homeland. Some Native Americans adopted European ways and joined the white settlers' **culture.**

The last Native American groups in Illinois lost their land to the United States government by 1833. They moved west across the Mississippi River to settle in Iowa, Kansas, and Oklahoma. The tribes settled in **reservations** set up there by the U.S. government.

Illinois tribes still hold traditional events, such as powwows (below), which help preserve their cultures.

Native American Reservations

On the reservation, Native Americans were expected to give up their tribe's old ways and religion. Instead, they were supposed to learn to live like white settlers. Native American children on the reservations were often sent to boarding schools. At these schools, they were not allowed to speak their tribal language or practice their **traditional** culture. As a result, some languages died out and some traditions were forgotten.

Most Native American tribes were eventually forced onto reservations by the United States government. Most Illinois tribes now have reservations in Oklahoma. Of course, Native Americans also live all over the United States.

Today, the tribes that once lived in Illinois maintain reservations, where some of their members live. Other members of those tribes live in cities or on privately owned farms. Native Americans everywhere are working to preserve their old ways. Tribes present powwows, which are celebrations of Native American dancing, music, food, and crafts. They make sound recordings and keep written records of their languages, so that they can be passed on to future generations. They also use **websites** and other modern technology to educate others about their **cultures.**

Native American tribes also try to provide their members with the chance to earn a good living. On many **reservations,** people are unable to work because there

Tribal-run casinos (right) have helped reservations earn money. The Ho-Chunk are a group of Winnebago that have returned to Wisconsin. They also used to live in Illinois. The group operates a bison ranch and prairie preserve in Wisconsin, too.

are not enough jobs to go around. Tribes operate businesses as part of the effort to create jobs. Many tribes have opened gambling **casinos** and other tourist attractions.

In 2000, there were more than 4 million Native Americans in the United States. Illinois is still home to about 31,000. They are members of tribes from all over North America. Many moved to Illinois to find jobs in cities.

They still try to preserve their **traditions.** Native Americans hold powwows in Chicago, Peoria, Utica, and other places in Illinois. Native American children participate as dancers, drummers, or storytellers.

Fox

The last Fox communities left Illinois by 1832. In 1867, the United States declared that the Fox and their neighbors the Sauk should be considered one tribe. The new tribe was called the Sac and Fox Nation. Today, about 400 members of the Sac and Fox Nation live on a reservation in Oklahoma. The tribe hosts a yearly powwow and runs a museum. Another group of Fox live in Iowa and call themselves the *Mesquakie*, which is their traditional name. The Mesquakie run a school that teaches Native American children about native culture.

Kickapoo

During the 1800s, the Kickapoo kept moving west to avoid white settlers. Eventually they settled in Kansas, Oklahoma, Texas, and Mexico. During their many moves they had to change some of their ways to match their new surroundings. For example, as they moved away from wooded areas, the Kickapoo wove baskets from reeds instead of bark. Today, there are three different groups of Kickapoo recognized by the U.S. government. The Kickapoo are known for their commitment to tribal traditions. About half of today's Kickapoo still speak the Kickapoo language.

This is now the official seal of the Sac and Fox Nation, which has a reservation in Oklahoma.

MIAMI

The Miami were pushed out of Illinois by 1833. In 1846, they split into two tribes: The Miami Tribe of Oklahoma and the Miami Nation of Indians of the State of Indiana. Today, the Miami Tribe of Oklahoma runs a racing track and **casino** on its **reservation.** The tribe also owns a farm and prairie preserve, where the Miami continue their **tradition** as skilled farmers. The Miami Nation of Indians of the State of Indiana puts on a yearly show illustrating the tribe's history. They are also working to buy back parts of the tribe's traditional homeland.

PEORIA

The Peoria sold the last of their land to the United States in 1832. They then settled in Kansas. In 1854, they merged with the Wea and Piankashaw, two tribes that had once been part of the Miami. In 1867, the Peoria moved to Oklahoma.

Chief Illiniwek

People have become more aware of how Native Americans were often mistreated by white settlers and the United States government in the past. As a result, many people want to get rid of sports **mascots** they now feel are disrespectful of Native American **cultures.** The University of Illinois's sports teams are named the Fighting Illini. They are named for the Illinois Nation, whose people were sometimes called the Illini. The university's mascot is Chief Illiniwek. He is known for the dance he performs at football and basketball games. Many people object to Chief Illiniwek. They say he and his dance are disrespectful of Illinois tribal culture and traditions. There has been a disagreement as to whether or not the mascot should be changed.

Today, all living **descendants** of the tribes of the Illinois Nation are represented by the Peoria. These include the Cahokia, Chepoussa, Chinko, Coiracoentanon, Espeminkia, Kaskaskia, Michibousa, Michigamea, Moingwena, Peoria, Tamaroa, and Tapouaro. The Peoria tribe has about 2,500 members in the United States. It is governed by an elected chief and a business **committee,** with tribal offices in Miami, Oklahoma. There it gives classes in traditional language and arts in order to help preserve the Peoria ways. It also hosts a yearly powwow and runs a golf course on tribal land in Oklahoma.

The Peoria run the Peoria Ridge Golf Course (above) on their tribal land in Oklahoma. The Peoria now includes the Kaskaskia, Peoria, Piankeshaw, and Wea tribes.

POTAWATOMI

The Treaty of Chicago of 1833 gave the last of the Potawatomi land in Illinois to the United States. The Potawatomi moved west across the Mississippi River and soon broke up into six bands, or groups. Today, Potawatomi live in Michigan, Wisconsin, Kansas, Oklahoma, and other states. The Potawatomi in Oklahoma operate a tribal museum, golf course, and other attractions. The Potawatomi in Wisconsin operate a large casino. In all, there are about 17,000 Potawatomi in the United States.

SAUK

After the Black Hawk War of 1832, the last Sauk communities were pushed out of Illinois. In 1867, the United

States government created the Sac and Fox Nation by merging the Sauk and their neighbors, the Fox. Today, the Sac and Fox Nation is based in Oklahoma. The tribe hosts a yearly powwow on its **reservation** and runs a museum.

SHAWNEE

The Shawnee were driven from their homelands in the early 1800s. They soon split into three tribes, each with its own reservation in Oklahoma and its own tribal government. The tribes are the Eastern Shawnee, the Absentee Shawnee, and the Loyal Shawnee. There is also a band of Shawnee in Ohio working to buy back pieces of the tribe's homelands.

WINNEBAGO

The Winnebago gave up all of their land east of the Mississippi River to the United States in 1829. The tribe moved west and settled on a reservation in Nebraska. Today, the Winnebago run a **casino** there and host a yearly powwow. Some Winnebago students attend Nebraska Indian Community College's Winnebago **campus.** Another group of Winnebago have returned to Wisconsin and call themselves Ho-Chunk, which means "people of the first voice." The group operates a **bison** ranch and prairie preserve in central Wisconsin.

Ho-Chunk means "people of the first voice." The name Winnebago was given to the Ho-Chunk by the Sauk and Fox. The group operates a bison ranch (right) and prairie preserve in central Wisconsin.

44

Timeline

20,000–10,000 B.C.E.	Paleo-Indians arrive in Illinois.
8000–1000 B.C.E.	People of the **Archaic Period** begin farming in Illinois.
1000 B.C.E.–C.E. 800	Woodland people introduce the bow and arrow to Illinois.
C.E. 900–1500	People of the **Mississippian Period** build large mounds along the Mississippi River.
1500	Tribes of the Illinois Nation control the Mississippi River valley.
1650s	The Iroquois invade Illinois territory.
1673	Marquette and Jolliet explore the Illinois and Mississippi Rivers.
1680	French explorer La Salle begins building **forts** along the Illinois River.
1756	The French and Indian War begins, matching Great Britain against France and its Native American **allies.**
1763	The French and Indian War ends. Illinois becomes British territory.
1775	The American Revolution begins.
1779	Jean Baptiste Pointe du Sable establishes a trading post at present-day Chicago.
1783	Great Britain turns the Illinois country over to the United States in the Treaty of Paris, at the end of the American Revolution.
1803	The Kaskaskia turn over lands east of the Mississippi River to the United States government.
1812	About 500 Native Americans attack Fort Dearborn.
1818	Illinois becomes a state. The Peoria give up their land to the U.S. government in the Treaty of Edwardsville.
1819	The Kickapoo move west of the Mississippi River.
1829	The Potawatomi give up their lands in northern Illinois.
1832	Black Hawk leads the last Native American resistance to white settlement in Illinois in the Black Hawk War. The Sauk and Fox are driven from Illinois.
1832	The Kaskaskia and Peoria settle on a reservation in Kansas.
1940	The Peoria Indian Tribe of Oklahoma is formed.

Glossary

ally person or group of people who promise to help someone else

archaeologist person who studies the way people once lived by examining objects left behind by people of the past

Archaic Period ca. 8000 B.C.E. to 1000 B.C.E. This is also sometimes broken up into the Early, Middle, and Late Archaic Periods, and dates sometimes differ among sources.

bison also sometimes called a buffalo; large, shaggy-maned mammal with short horns and a hump

breechcloth piece of clothing worn around the midsection

campus land around a college

casino building used for entertainments such as card games

ceremony act or set of acts done in a certain way to celebrate a special occasion

Christianity religion that came from Jesus Christ and is based on the Bible; Eastern, Roman Catholic, and Protestant churches are Christian, as are members of those churches

clan group of families descended from a common ancestor

climate weather conditions that can be found in a certain area

committee group of people who are chosen to do something

council group of people who meet to decide important matters or to give advice

culture ideas, skills, arts, and way of life of a certain people at a certain time

descendant person whose family background can be traced to a certain individual or group

elder older person who helps lead a community

extinct no longer living

fast go without food for a period of time

fertile bearing crops or vegetation in abundance

fort strong building used for defense against enemy attack

herb plant with parts that are used as medicine or to flavor food

Ice Age period of time when a large part of the earth was covered with glaciers and the temperatures were cooler

lacrosse game played by many Native American peoples, in which two teams try to propel a ball into a goal

mammoth large, extinct animal, similar to an elephant, with shaggy hair and long tusks

mascot emblem or representative of a school's athletic teams

mastodon large, extinct animal, similar to an elephant, with tusks and shaggy hair

missionary person sent by a church to spread his or her religious beliefs; a mission is a place where missionaries live and work

Mississippian Period Native American culture that existed between C.E. 500 and 1500

moccasin shoe made of soft leather made from deerskins

pelt skin taken from an animal

plaza public square in a city or town

prehistoric from the time before history was written

quill large, stiff feather from the wing or tail of a bird; also one of the sharp, stiff spines that stick out on the body of a porcupine

reservation area of public land set apart for use by Native American tribes

ritual set of actions performed as part of a religious ceremony

rush grasslike plant with hollow stems found in wet places such as marshes

sacred bundle animal-skin pouch that contains objects representing glorious moments in the history of a clan or tribe

shaman Native American believed to have special healing powers and the ability to communicate with the spirits

sinew tough band of tissue that connects muscles with bones

spiritual of the spirit or soul, apart from the body or material world; also having to do with religion

tepee tent made of animal skins surrounding long poles and shaped like a cone

tradition custom or belief that is handed down from generation to generation

vision quest right of manhood (part of becoming a man) in which a Native American boy tries to communicate with spirits by fasting (not eating) for a period of time

website particular electronic address on the World Wide Web, which is used to move around on the Internet. You can find information about an organization or company on their website.

wigwam dome-shaped Native American hut with a frame of poles covered with bark, rush mats, or animal hides

Woodland Period ca. 1000 B.C.E. to C.E. 750. This is also sometimes broken up into the Early, Middle, and Late Woodland Periods, and dates sometimes differ among sources.

More Books to Read

Hunter, Sally M. *Four Seasons of Corn: A Winnebago Tradition.* Minneapolis, Minn.: Lerner Publishing, 1996.

Marsh, Carole. *Illinois Indians: A Kid's Look at Our State's Chiefs, Tribes, Reservations, Powwows, Lore and More From the Past and the Present!* Peachtree City, Ga.: Gallopade, 1997.

McDaniel, Melissa. *The Sac and Fox Indians.* Broomall, Pa.: Chelsea House, 1997.

Powell, Suzanne. *The Potawatomi.* New York: Franklin Watts, 1998.

Sherrow, Victoria. *American Indian Children of the Past.* Brookfield, Conn.: Millbrook Press, 1997.

Fiction:

Curry, Jane Louise. *Turtle Island: Tales of the Algonquin Nations.* New York: Simon and Schuster Children's, 1999.

Wooldridge, Jack. *Jomin's Lamp: A Potawatomi Fable.* Santa Cruz, Calif.: Pota Press, 1997.

Index

About the Author

Andrew Santella lives in Trout Valley, Illinois, and is a lifelong resident of the state of Illinois. He is the author of 25 nonfiction books for children. He also writes for publications such as *GQ* and the *New York Times Book Review*.